HOSIERY SEAMS
ON A BOWLEGGED WOMAN

poems by Thylias Moss

Cleveland State University Poetry Center

Photos of Thylias Moss on the front cover and the inside
covers are by John Moss.

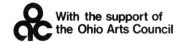

With the support of
the Ohio Arts Council

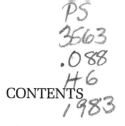

CONTENTS

The straight lines of a Greek temple are delicately curved to look straighter still.

— F. L. Lucas

ALTERNATIVES FOR A CELIBATE DAUGHTER

1.

This man is going to die without telling me.
It will happen while I dream of tornadoes
those frantic clouds swirling in search of mates.
I won't be caught without a man
to order my life like an alphabet:
Albert   Bernard   Clifford   Desmond   Eric   Father's
going to die but I'm afraid
to hold his hand. If I feel something
daughters shouldn't feel   I won't let go.

2.

I don't choose men wisely.
When all else failed I went to father.
Now he ignores me. He will not answer.
I shake him and he hardens into slate,
cold, smooth. What can I do?
I'm a trained daughter
yet the wreath I carry
could double as a bride's bouquet.

3.

The dream, almost a year old.
In it, his name for me is a flower: Hyacinth,
a final pink breath.

FROM THE BRIDE'S JOURNAL

1.
The room fills, refills
without emptying. The light
is dusty and old. His will
holds the wood together, thoughts
compress logs into planks.
Cracks aren't wide enough
for whispers. Cobwebs hang
like pontoon bridges
from one wall to the next.

2.
There's something of a coast
in his profile,
some poached country
where winds knock down trees
and undress them.

3.
The old DeSoto won't start.
I stare through the windshield.
We don't really resemble
the couple in the brochure
as my family suggested.

4.
In the cabin
I sit across from him
keeping on my hat, coat.
He says nothing,
removes my full plate from the table,
takes it outdoors, throws it,
shoots it.

He cracks his knuckles
in the doorway, shakes off snow,
carries me over his shoulder.
His zipper sounds like a saw.

THE BARREN MIDWIFE SPEAKS OF DUTY

I must get on with it. Children
aren't aware how close their mothers
come to death, as close as the sky
comes to earth at night: they touch.
The supine women aren't pretty;
how they look when it's over,
how pensile their paunches become,
like a milch cow's dewlap
and just as useless.
Second trimester bellies parade
outside my window. I want to shout:
you got that way without my help;
leave me alone. Instead
I don't even complain when the oilcloth
is stained.

I have the best job, bringing them into the world
then I'm through. Childbirth pains
foreshadow what's to come. Knowing that
I should shove the heads back,
stitch the openings.
Instead I teach these women a lesson.

LIFE IN A STERILE ENVIRONMENT: A CASE STUDY

1.
Manna must be pried
from the road. A towheaded boy
helps me. We're a couple:
mother/son, father/daughter,
lovers. The mind is made
to accept so much, truth
we couldn't possibly verify
except to point out
new hairs around my nipples.
All growth will have to come
from within. These rocks
are not unlike the puffball cakes
I sprinkled sugar over
on holidays.

2.
We pile manna on my skirt.
I'm only ashamed of not being much
to look at. Once
I dreamt of stripping
in front of Hajek's Bakery,
lying prone on hot cobblestone
until officers covered me
with a sheet.

The boy thinks only of manna,
should we eat it raw
or cooked. Should we save some
or is it true the supply's inexhaustible.
I give him a piece, he won't swallow it,
won't be greedy in this time of plenty.
He can't remember ever having more,

not in the last hundred years.
He'd forgotten how long he'd lived,
how much he'd eaten: can't die
or starve. He throws the manna,
hands me my skirt.
There's something eternal at work,
not the long-sought peace but   absence.

3.
We sketch birds in the dirt,
stare at them till they fly away
then we thank any idea of God
that remains in the rubble
of St. Andrew's,
holding hands so tightly
we break the nails;
yes, we were good parents,
he tells me, staring at the empty sky,
we let go.

He leads me to the fishmonger's stall:
interpreter, tour guide, seeing eye,
composer of epitaphs.
Here, steel-and-brick-hued carp
shined like new money.
That's when you buy,
after the ice under them melts,
after they stink. A good price then.

He spins a wheel of the overturned cart,
starts the monger's steely voice.
"Love for sale." *Buy it,* I plead.
"Going once." *Buy it.* "Going twice."
"Gone."

4. Final observations

The couple who has everything
leaves the stall, hugging the stinking
parcel, passing it between them.
From a distance they're like
hosiery seams on a bowlegged woman.
After sunset they pale
into the thinnest glass,
weigh less than reflexions.
Small crucifixes on filigree chains
fall through them.

LOST CHILDREN

1.
You know how the sun looks
when half of it tears the sky,
the reds and oranges, the hurt
of rising and setting,
how swollen it looks
as if with child?
It was like that when Pepita told me
to pretend she wasn't made of air,
that she wouldn't gust soon.
I haven't seen her since.

That's the way it is with fever.

2.
Now it's enough for me to come out of the house
once a day, sit on the grass, bear down on it
with the full weight of my seventy-eight years.
The blades under me knit into a pattern like the
cross-stitch of my fingers. I'm an old woman.
I'm thought penitent because my left hand keeps
embracing, locking with the right when really
it's because of things like kneading,
the constant kneading, wanting to be original
but not escaping the pregnant shape of loaves.
Lengthy labors that don't produce a child.

3.
I'm ashamed to go to market
without the children.
I'm emptyhanded. I've nothing to sell.
Behind me once there were long lines
of children. Always
and when we walked the line shook
like a proud flag.

4.
It's a fact.
Every day a child is lost.
There are statistics. For some reason
they don't like it here.
One child in particular;
sometimes I see her face
so clearly. No, she was never me.

OLD MAIDS WEAVING BASKETS

I was with you when Valhermosa
was a river, when we held hands
to fight the current,
came ashore, couldn't let go,
huddled in the church-like
shadow of Edna's house
and weathervane. Valhermosa's
a creek now, an unjoined seam,
lovers reaching.

We met under this linden
the day Edna married her cousin,
honeymooned up north.
From her yard she could see
everything: two sets
of underwear on a limb.
You got here first, hid
behind branches, a bride
helped by veil. Bared breasts
filled your bowl of a lap.

Today's no different.
Deliberately I kept you waiting
till Edna left the window.
Despite rumors
we have those baskets,
a respectable business.
Your feet dangle, insect bites
on both ankles, while we plait
grasses, sapwood cuttings:
motions learned from breaking
blessed bread.

Later we collect berries
in the freshly made baskets,
eat from each other's hand,
tremble,
echoes fearing error.
You said a man
would leave you.

DOWN TO THE LAST DOMINO

1.

Dice come clean in his hands,
all dots and periods erased
to clarify meaning
down to smooth, white cubes,
perfect though lacking
the curve of hips.

2. Hips

However long hands are on them,
they can't be pushed in,
they aren't retractable:
they remain hips.
He has more respect
for hips
than the clean dice
though dice
have all the right angles.

3. Right angles

Ninety degrees is an uncomfortable
temperature. Somewhere
he's sure it's ninety degrees right now.
Somewhere a wife is beaten.
He's certain these events are related.
It's always been right to blame
the weather, to hear the weatherman
mention heat, humidity
before the news can be understood
in context.

4. Context

Start with the body,
the overheated body,
constant 98.6.
He will stay indoors,
drawn curtains, dark glasses
until he cools down
and is safe to touch.

THINGS YET UNREACHABLE

Undressing with his back to me
he stares out the window
searching for gaps in the horizon,
places where earth and sky don't come together,
an excuse not to come to me.
There's got to be a limit
to excuses, eventually they must run out,
the way a wife one night admits
the extra blanket
hasn't stopped the cold.
He could concentrate and avoid
repetition: the zipper up and down
like a puny motor failing to catch,
a mistake made over and over
until it feels wrong to break
what is now tradition.
His crippled leg, not quite a mystery.
He's forgotten our first year,
the table's unevenness, the wobble
typical of things at sea.
Paper captain's hat from the *Daily News*,
homemade maps spread out,
missions plotted with protractors, rulers.
He was responsible for the war.
I can't ignore the mounting evidence,
possible explanations
for why he fumbles with buttons:
in the last light his hands seem webbed
as if what's attached to them
should be pelicans or gulls
that sound like him
weeping in the morning
when they risk dives.

ONE TAKEN BY BANDITS

There's no way to feel but illegitimate.
Christ was — Mary never married God.
June: the last time I shaved my legs,
plucked my brows. Bandits don't mind
such hairiness, unchallenged as cacti spines.
Maybe that's why they don't touch me.
They suck marrow from pork bones.
Tequila, in trickles, washes their chins.
I wouldn't mind that they've confused me
with a blessed virgin
except it's no blessing being a virgin.
Nor is it a foolproof contraceptive,
look what happened to Mary.
Such terrible nights,
nine available arms don't reach for me,
not even a quick gesture
like a lizard's shy tongue
though my blouse is always open.
Insomnia makes me notice how stars
rearrange themselves or disappear
into the nearest black hole. Beside me:
the bandit without teeth.
Husband, I gasp, rolling over.

I THINK ABOUT HOW EASILY SHADOWS FUSE

Rebecca Robinson died on my birthday.
She hung around Jew ladies,
hardly ever went to church
since that Sunday
she saw the funnel cloud
forming above True Vine Baptist.
It never did swoop down
or suck up any of the loose bricks
that were the church's steps.

True Vine was always Baptist,
its Bibles used to be Hungarian
and ladies who wore doilies
on their pee-colored hair
used to be silent in the services.
The pews sag
where their wide fannies dimpled them.

I get there before anyone else,
crawl through the basement's
broken window to get in. Upstairs
I look at Rebecca's old seat
on the mourners' bench:
she didn't make an impression.
Then I go to the piano, press one white key
and copy the note,
filling the place
with my voice, filling the cracks.

Rebecca's my name too, middle name.
I'll probably die like the other Rebecca
and leave behind
a shoebox of unanswered letters

from people I'd like to remember.
Memory can prove existence.
That's why the bench worries me,
why I give my voice to the cracks.
After I'm gone
the walls will scream.

A CHILD'S BEEN DEAD A WEEK

We take turns
dressing her, propping her
by the window facing the street.
Our miracle is so simple:
a fresh-laid egg — still warm,
cradled against a cheek
then boiled in vinegar,
is opened a little,
taken to an anthill
and buried.
When the egg is consumed
completely, she revives.

We're not welcome in the church.
I get as far as the vestibule,
can even hear the hymns.
An usher opens the door for me.
We only need a *simple* prayer:
Lord, make the ants eat.

ST. ALEXIS HOSPITAL: VISITING HOUR

I ask if she remembers
when she thought nuns never died.
I haven't seen a dead one yet,
she replies.

From under the bed she pulls out
a trunk full of rosaries.
End to end, they cover a mile.

Then off comes the heavy black skirt
and I tuck her in,
shake crumbs from her missal,
turn off the lamp, let the same
darkness touch us.

She tells me about the crazy nun
who wanted to grow wings,
that every night she massaged
her back with lilies' dew
and Mary's milk.

They can't get her temperature
down.

GOODNESS AND THE SALT OF THE EARTH

Somebody's husband raped you while you were supposed to be in the choir pounding a tambourine, not a chest. Early Sunday morning, must have been an Easter Sunday because something came back from death, it came with a wedding ring and it was black and it smiled and it was good. You got pregnant. Good. Had an abortion. Good. That's what the Lord said in Genesis, he saw the world and what was happening, and it was still good. So you were good and turned the pages, read every line, and Lot's wife, that good woman, turned to salt because she was polite and couldn't leave without saying good-bye. You said it in the hospital: "Good-bye, baby, you never cried, just ate salt and died, just got tossed over the left shoulder. You broke. I never got a chance to see myself in you." In church the sisters shouted, fainted. O hallelujah! O the glory! Ushers came running, *smell the salt, sister; smell the salt.* Sometimes it brings you back. Sometimes it kills. Don't trust it. Stay away from bacon, ham, all cured meat. Stay away from uncles licking palms so the salt sticks. Stay away from men. Stay away from angry crowds yelling, "Salt, Peter. Salt, Peter." Ask the Saint for something else. It always rains. It always pours. Thank goodness.

DENIAL

This is supposed to be a denial. The Millers say I stole their toddler. The wife adds that precious wasn't even weaned. I'm supposed to say I never saw the child and that the only Millers I know is beer. I'm supposed to slap my thigh, act like a jolly lesbian who would, if she thought about stealing a toddler, give more consideration to gender. These Millers have a hyperactive boy. I'm told. I'm supposed to say I only resemble the Salvation Army general who rescues kids from abusive and burning homes. I have one of those faces that keeps turning up in newspapers, the police artist's composite sketch. I'm supposed to guffaw at irregular intervals. I'm supposed to hoist my feet on top of the desk and create a sensation by being crass and crude. On the advice of my lawyer I'm not supposed to plead insanity just demonstrate it.

The truth is I kept the baby while they vacationed. The truth is I won their child as payment for their poker debts. The truth is I'm the surrogate and I decided to keep the child. The truth is I had the child. Look at the womb print. I had the child but I lost it. The truth is I'm hooked up to this machine — lie detector, kidney dialysis, cathode ray decoder, automatic D & C and waxer, trying to get the nurse to overdose my morphine. Trying.

ABOUT FLAGS

First there must be thunder,
lightning must dissolve
in Father's bourbon
then he passes it around
with a snapshot, saying
"remember Ira Hamilton Hayes
and the war that made him
a hero. One Pima
that never sold pottery
or let a child stick a pigeon
feather in his unbraided hair
for a dollar."

Fifteen years and I can't
like the taste but drain
the bottle anyway.
Though I'm not Pima.
In me Choctaw and Cherokee mix
with unnamed African tribes.
My great-grandmother still said *slave*
in 1961   like it was a country.

Others think you did nothing
for your people but I
look at Father's copy
of that award-winning photo,
flag-raising on Iwo Jima;
your hand doesn't touch the pole.
I know you could have,
had you wanted,
that pole wasn't out of reach
but the hawk — one of your flags
raises itself.

SPRING CLEANING AT THE LEWISTON POLICE STATION

In the basement,
a box of human bones
dug up
near the Camas Prairie Railroad Bridge
by accident.
The police were just
doing their job
when they put the bones
in a box
in the basement
and forgot them
for nine years.
A preliminary report in 1971
indicated the bones
may have belonged
to an Indian woman.
No definite opinion
could be obtained
since the bones
couldn't speak.
The University of Idaho
has them now.
If the bones
are Indian bones,
they'll go to the Nez Perce tribe,
if they are not,
they'll go back in the box.

ONE-LEGGED COOK

A high school cafeteria
is where I work. "Hop to it, Velma,"
kids say when the line moves slow.
My son eats outdoors from a bag,
collar turned up, napkin
covering his knees.
That's what I live with.
Never occurred to me
I was missing out on something.
Though seldom seem in Culvert Hall
I know to sit still
when the conductor taps his stick;
my father waved a strap.
Besides, it doesn't take that much,
the burdock by the courthouse
grew an eighth of an inch
since yesterday.
A lot of folks didn't notice.

RUSH HOUR

He boards the train downtown,
same time I get on in Lee Heights.

Eastbound passes westbound.
Can't pick him out,

square-shouldered every one of them,
under 40 years old, over 40 thousand a year,

never glancing up from their papers
till they pass Quincy, Central Avenue's

gutted brownstones, record and head shops,
Joe D's Tavern where I rent the back room.

He's ashamed of what we have in common.
I just left his house. Spotless.

FIVE MIRACLES

for S.A.B., Z.N.H., L.H., C.H., M.H., et al.

1.
We were cutting corn from cobs,
separating pied kernels
into red piles, yellow, black.
We weren't told to do this.
We took it upon ourselves
to make distinctions,
showing off our mother wit:
red into bowls,
yellow into jars with dated labels,
black into the scuttle
by the stove.

2.
Lutie Watson swallowed a snake
when she drank at the creek
that lynchers sank Jo-jo's stone-filled
body in last year;
that snake must have been
his soul transformed
because now she's pregnant again,
way past the age of possibility.

3.
Went to a gypsy.
Gypsy had never seen a lifeline so long.
Stretches from my thumb to my shoulder.

4.
He may be a buck-toothed
ugly dude

but he ain't a sawed-off runt.
Shoulders so broad
looks like his head
sits on a boxcar.
I go walking with him
through them I-talian sections,
them Polish and what-have-you sections,
people damn near bow.
His T-shirt (special made) says:
Home-grown in Darkest Africa.

5.
What's a *nice* colored girl like you
doing in New England?
Thinking about changing my reputation.

THE DAY BEFORE KINDERGARTEN: TALUCA, ALABAMA, 1959

I watch daddy tear down
Mama Lelia's outhouse
with just his hands;
the snakes and slugs
didn't fret him none.
Then he takes me and mama riding.

We stop at the store,
looks like a house,
okra right in front,
chickpeas and hollyhocks.
Me and mama go in. The fan
don't move her hair.
She keeps her head down, stands
a long time at the counter.
Just wants some thread,
could get it herself,
there's a basketfull beside her.
Clerk keeps reading.

She's hurting my wrist,
I pull away, pick up a doll.
Clerk says we have to leave.
Mama grabs me and runs
right by daddy,
he's just coming in.

We hide in the car.
Mama smells like sour milk
and bleach.
Daddy comes out toting a sack,
clerk thought he was white.

When the store starts burning
I'm on Mama Lelia's porch
wanting to see
how the red
melts off peppermint.
I know it's like that.
One by one
each thing burns.
Pickle jars explode.
Mama Lelia asks me:
do it look like rain?
No'm, it don't.
Ain't God good!
She laughs.

Later,
while it's still smoking
I go poking with a stick.
Ashes look like nappy
nigger hair. Smells
like when the hot comb
gets too hot
and burns mama's neck.
This smell's so big
must have come
from a hundred necks.

Holding my doll
I look at the smoke,
could be a black man
running down the road;
then rub some ashes
on her face
cause I ain't scared
no more
of nothing.
Maybe I should be
but I ain't.

TALUCA, TWENTY YEARS LATER

Its one road leads out of town,
have to go the wrong way
to get there.

SOME HISTORY, SOME PROPHECY, SOME TRUTH

1.
Me and Skan both know he ain't black.
He *Crow* but he do look
most white. I tell him
to keep that *Crow* stuff secret
cause that makes these niggers
uneasy. So Skan's passing.

Course I never did find out
what a *nigger-lover* was,
I still been fixed on *indian-giver*;
now that seem a might respectable thing.
Seem to me them indians give up
all they land. They mammies must pluck
every selfish hair from they heads.
I be right proud
if somebody call me a *indian-giver*;
they the ones gon see heaven,
not the ones the indians
given it to.

And hell, guess I been a *nigger-lover*
all a my natural life,
cause I sho do loves me some
niggers, a whole mess a them,
lined up right in front a my doorstep,
wearing NIGGER banners
cross they puffed out chests.
The more nigger they look
the better, like gorillas. *Real*
niggerish.

Don't hear tell a *redneck-lover*
cause that don't much exist.

Me and Skan do our loving in the open,
we be hoping somebody see us.
Don't worry bout no lynching.
Skan pat his thigh. He say:
I got my .38 with me.
He don't mean a gun.

2.
They was glad when my mama got pregnant.
Cause of Skan she could lighten up the family.
Soon's they crossed the Mason-Dixon line,
mama's pains started coming. Said that
was a sign. Told Skan to keep heading north
till the baby comes. It'll know where
it wants to be born. Seems I chose Cleveland.
That means something too.
But I'm almost the same color she is.
Can't tell to look at me that the color ain't pure.
Still, they know since I got it in me
it got to come out — my daughter's taffy-colored
though I married the blackest man I could find.

3.
Course, it don't bother me
that I can't trace my mama's family
further back than 1861
when my great grand-mama's
mama was born. Seems
I can most shake hands with slavery,
that's too close for me.
Thought it happened *long* ago.
Knew my great-grandmama
till I was thirteen,
had tits big as kumquats by then,
almost as grown as I was ever gon get.

Sometimes I didn't like
how she look at me.
Said I could get anything I wanted.
Master would a wanted to sleep with me,
I got the right kind a hair,
I ain't quite dark enough to be ugly.
I'd get dark if I worked in the field!
"He won't let you," she'd say.
Then I spend hours
trying to flatten my nose.

She tells me:
don't write things down
cause then it belongs to the paper.
Keep it safe inside.
Best to pass information
like blood through veins.
Too dangerous
to have pieces of evidence.
That's why the indians tell
they stories too.

4.
You know how niggers are.
We think everything means something.
If Aunt Irene is the first to our house
on New Year's day, she got to stay outdoors
in the sleet, the rain, the whatever
until a man comes in
unless we ain't too particular
bout the kind a luck we gon have,
Cat can steal a baby's breath.
Hand itching means money,
foot means you need a bath.

So it means something
that I'm the first in the family
to go to college.
When I walked cross that stage
for the diploma
I had to count my steps:
one for each relative.
They count too, seeing
would anybody be left out.
No. College must a learned me
to count real good.

I tell them I'm gon work
on a Master's degree
and they think I'm getting
religion. I say *phibetakappa*
they think I'm speaking in tongues.

They don't like me to use nigger-talk,
talk proper round us,
maybe it'll rub off.
They don't understand.
Every now and then
I have to use it,
least so I don't forget.
When I'm mad I use it.
When I talk love-talk I use it.
I use it wid a voice
that sound like something
the wind could easily push around
yet can't move.
Lord, if it don't try.

I know it's dangerous
to write this, but

whatever's in me got to come out.
The joy, cause it's in there too
and the rest.
No moth's gon dawdle
by a not-there flame.
Lordy, Lordy, look at me!
I do declare I'm being smothered
by wings.